Tanzanite Career
Development Services (TCDS)

# Manual for College Programme Choices

Pancras K. MAYENGO

*For Ordering Information visit www.tcds.or.tz*

Print    *ISBN 978-1-9163720-5-4*
eBook    *ISBN 978-1-9163720-6-1*

*First edition*

# TABLE OF CONTENTS

# ACKNOWLEDGEMENTS

This manual is a result of thorough discussions and brainstorming with my colleague and a close partner in Career Development Services, Mr. Elias J. Mwinuka. He has influenced my thinking in great measures. Before meeting him, I would ask children, "What do you want to be when you grow up?" But now, I ask, "Why do you want to be what you want to be?"

The contents of the rationale of this manual, the career pathways and the self-assessment career exploration is a result of his dialogue and guidance. I would be heartless if I do not acknowledge his contribution.

# Chapter 1

# INTRODUCTION

## 1.1 Rationale for this Manual

Many young people have little knowledge about social problems and their respective causes. As a result, they fail to establish which occupations are key to solving those problems. Hence, their career aspirations are not in alignment with future work demands.

This manual will expose young people to different social problems and help them determine which ones they would like to solve when they grow up. Such awareness is what leads to a purposeful existence.

It is of utmost importance you ask why you want to be in a certain occupation before you decide what you want to be. The justification of what you want to be should base on solving social economic problems in your society. Thereafter, you need to choose college programmes that may equip you with technical skills to execute proficiently the duties of your prospective job.

Unfortunately most young people lack skills of selecting academic courses related to their career aspirations due to various reasons:

i. They just look to pass and how they have scored in the Form Six examination rather than being based on their career aspirations.

ii. They select university programmes based on the availability of financial assistance from Higher Education Students' Loans Board (HESLB).

iii. Caregivers influence career selection based on their preferences of some occupations that they had wished to be in but due to various reasons they couldn't. Thus, there's peer influence on the course selection.

iv. Unsuccessful people in labour market who took certain courses.

## 1.2 Our Approach

Based on the challenges that young people face, as highlighted above, this manual addresses the challenges through the following:

i. Creating self-awareness of the applicants in terms of the strengths, interests and career aspirations.

ii. Future of work and how the world of work is changing.

iii. Knowing the different career options available in the labour market.

iv. Understanding different academic pathways.

v. Developing an action plan to achieve their career goals.

## 1.3 Purpose

The purpose of this manual is to guide A-level leavers and equivalent applicants such as certificate and diploma applicants to accurately choose university programmes that are aligned to their career aspirations.

## 1.4 Target Audience

This manual is relevant for anyone, including the following, who would like to guide, train, counsel and coach others in the areas of career choice and development:

    i. Policymakers
    ii. Parents and caregivers
    iii. Students
    iv. Colleges and universities
    v. Profit and non-profit organisations supporting young people in post-secondary education
    vi. Anyone joining academic institution for a course
    vii. Career development practitioners

## 1.5 Composition

The composition here refers to the "configuration management strategy" in the profession of project planning and management. Hence, this manual and the training package thereafter, will compose skills and knowledge of:

1. What career jobs are available in different economic sectors?
2. What factors influence these career jobs over time?
3. Understand where the world of work is going.
4. What are the available university or college programmes?
5. Career planning, goal setting, for what you want to be?

6. University or college admission information, including where, when to do online applications, course information, course objectives, course entrance requirements, application requirements, dates of courses, date of approval or rejection notification, re-appeal or re-application.
7. Hands-on doing for online applications and career planning.
8. Financial assistance information including:
    a. Access to information about student loan programmes and long- term implications.
    b. Listings of scholarships, bursaries, grants, and other student assistance programmes or funds.
    c. Access to financial planning and debt management information.
    d. Access to financial literacy information and coaching.

Chapter 2

# OCCUPATIONAL PATHWAYS

## 2.1 Introduction

We define a job as a set of tasks and duties performed, or meant to be performed, by a person, whether they are employed or self-employed. Occupation is also defined as a set of jobs whose main tasks and duties are characterised by a high degree of similarity ("The International Labour Office" 2012).

By the end of this chapter, the reader will be able to answer the following questions:

    i.  What are the different occupations available in agriculture, industry and service sectors?

    ii.  What jobs interest you the most? What job would you like to do and in what sector?

    iii.  What professional skills do you require to do the job?

    iv.  What university courses can you pursue to get the required skills?

These questions intend to build your capacity to have a good understanding of what occupations are available in the world of work. Having a good knowledge of different career jobs is crucial in deciding what you would like to be in. In the following sections, we introduce you to different economic sectors and areas of specialisation.

## 2.2  Main Economic Sectors

For learning purposes, we assume that all economic activities can be grouped into three main groups; let's call them sectors. These are agriculture, industry and services.

The agriculture sector comprises all activities which are associated with agriculture, food and natural resources such as crop and livestock farming, fishing and forestry. Whereas the industry encompasses manufacturing and non-manufacturing activities. The manufacturing industry takes all agro and non-agro processing. The non-manufacturing industry includes all construction and architecture, mining activities and electricity as well as water supply.

All other activities that cannot be termed as agriculture or industry, fall under the services sector. These include the arts, business management and administration, human and health services, education and training, finance, information and technology, transportation, distribution and logistics, hospitality and tourism, marketing and government and public administration, among others.

**TABLE 2.2:** Economic Sectors and Occupational Pathways

| Main Sector | Sub-Sector | Occupational Pathways |
|---|---|---|
| Agriculture | | Crops & livestock, farming, fishing and forestry. |
| Industry | Manufacturing | Agro-processing & non-agro-processing |
| | Non-manufacturing | Architecture, construction and mining<br>Electricity production, transmission and supply<br>Water supply, sewage and waste control |
| Services | | Arts, audio-video technology and communications,<br>Business management and administration,<br>education and training,<br>Finance,<br>government and public administration,<br>hospitality and tourism,<br>human services,<br>information technology,<br>law, public safety, corrections and security,<br>marketing,<br>science, technology, engineering and mathematics,<br>transportation, distribution and logistics |

Source: International Standard Industrial Classification, (2008)

To be able to plan well, it is important to know beforehand the sector in which you are interested. You will need to do a career exploration of these sectors and meet different professionals in their places of works. At TCDS, we will prepare a package on career exploration where children will be introduced to these sectors in the early stages of their lives. You may visit us at www.tcds.or.tz to find out about other services that we offer. Further, an alternative to understanding the sectors is to study the occupations in these sectors which we explain in the following section.

## 2.3 Jobs and Occupations

After you understand the different economic sectors, you will need to understand the various occupations and jobs in the sectors.

A person can hold different jobs that still fall in one occupation. In  each job, the person applies different skills to perform the tasks and duties. Therefore, skills are the abilities to carry out the tasks and the duties of a given job. For the purpose of this manual, we use skill and competence interchangeably. However, we are aware that competence is much broader than skills.

According to the ILO Classification of Occupations, there are 10 major groups:

    i. Managers
    ii. Professionals
    iii. Technicians and associate professionals
    iv. Clerical support workers
    v. Services and sales workers
    vi. Skilled agricultural, forestry and fishery workers
    vii. Craft and related trades workers
    viii. Plant and machine operators and assemblers
    ix. Elementary occupations
    x. Armed forces occupations

These are further broken down into different occupations. We give an in-depth analysis of occupations during our in-house training, we have also prepared an online occupations database for you to practice (available on www.tcds.or.tz).

Normally, job adverts are very specific about who they want to employ. However, if one is not well-trained in these specialisations, one may apply for any vacancy, provided it is on finance, without knowing that there are different specialisations even in finance.

# 2.4 Key Competences of Specialisations

After you know the sector and the career pathway you would like to specialise in, the next step would be to identify key competencies required to perform the specific job. If you do the first two, that is identifying the sector and specialisation, and cannot identify the key competencies, it will be a drawback for you.

## 2.4.1 What is Professional Competence?

According to Borgonovo, Friedrich and Wells, "Competence is the ability to execute, in the real world, relevant tasks to a specified level of proficiency" (2019). So, you may know and understand a certain occupation, but that alone does not make you competent in the field. Competency requires that you effectively apply the relevant skills and particular attributes, which is usually only possible after undertaking specific practical experience.

## 2.4.2 Competence Vs. Knowledge-based Education

When employers advertise for a vacancy, they look for someone with competences to do the job. Unfortunately, many of our educational trainings do not prepare us for that. Most of the trainings are knowledge-based and only a few are competence-based. This can be understood by looking at the contrast between the two approaches.

Competence-based education focuses on developing competence rather than just knowledge. Similarly, competence-based training and certification go beyond imparting and requiring knowledge and focus on developing and requiring demonstration of desired tasks and outcomes at predetermined levels of proficiency.

**TABLE 2.4:** Competence vs knowledge-based education

| Knowledge-based Education | Competence-based Education |
|---|---|
| 1. Tests "Do you know how to …?" | 1. Tests "Can you. ..?" |
| 2. Focuses on what principles, concepts, facts or procedures to be learned | 2. Focuses on what tasks or outcomes need to be demonstrated |
| 3. Focuses on theory and concepts | 3. Focuses on the practical application of theory |
| 4. Sets minimum pass marks for percentage of knowledge that needs to be learned and sufficiently conveyed in assessments | 4. Sets minimum proficiency levels to be attained and demonstrated to be deemed competent for a role |
| 5. Often includes rote learning and tests memory | 5. Includes hands-on learning and active engagement, tests application of knowledge and skills in relevant contexts |

Source: Table 1.1 of Borgonovo, Friedrich, and Wells (2019)

## 2.4.3 Strategies for Developing Competences

### i. Volunteerism

Young people need to find places where they can start volunteering in different workplaces to develop their professional competence.

### ii. Internship

Though many internship opportunities for students or trainees in an organisation are sometimes without pay, it gives you an opportunity to gain work experience and improve your competences.

### iii. Field attachment

This can help develop professional competence if the host institution has strategies in place to support students during their presence in the institution as part of field attachment.

## 2.4.4 Skills for Developing Professional Competences

Soft skills are needed to complement professional development. These skills are key to succeed in labour market in the 21st century:

    i.   Social and emotional skills
    ii.  High-order thinking skills
   iii.  Digital skills
   iv.  Entrepreneurship skills

## 2.4.5 Education System and Competences

Unfortunately, most education systems do not prepare youngsters for acquiring professional competences but focus only on technical knowledge. Graduates are required to enrol in internships or field attachment programmes to gain professional competences. However, we feel that these remedial programmes cannot solve the problem.

The logic is simple: the increasing number of graduates will escalate the demand for internship positions. In the long run, this cannot be sustainable, unless the internship turns into training institutions. We, therefore, think that the best way is to integrate both technical knowledge and competence training in the education system.

This manual thus aims to raise awareness about choosing courses and training institutions that can impart skills and competences in performing specific job roles in the market. Having this knowledge will make youths concentrate on acquiring not only technical knowledge but also skills and competences, after getting enrolled in any training institution.

If you are given a choice between a training institution that teaches academic knowledge and another one that teaches technical skills and competences, you must choose the latter. This is because the working environment requires someone who can get the job done with a high standard; your competences will help you achieve that better as compared to only knowledge.

## 2.5  What Shapes Career Overtime

It is important to note that the changes in science and technology cause highly dramatic changes in many other occupations. It is also likely that the jobs of today might cease to exist in the future.

Consider the following examples of how technological advancement affects different occupations: postal mail services because of e-mails, engineering professions because of robots, traditional taxi services because of Uber, agriculture vs machines, legal profession because of artificial intelligence and records management because of e-government.

So, the future can bring completely new types of jobs where work will be conducted in a truly connected world. Jobs can become increasingly virtual and might be performed anywhere at any time. Employment could also shift to part-time and contractual work.

Therefore, understanding how different occupations change over time is crucial in planning what you want to be in the future.

## 2.6  Where is the World of Work Going?

We know that the future of work will run in the medium of automation and that most of the work available today will be replaced by machines in the near future. As a result, a generation of new jobs will emerge which will be at the interface of humans and automation.

What services do you think humans and robots will need in the future? Humans will still have the basic needs of shelter, clothing and food to survive, while robots will need to be programmed, serviced and re-inverted to come back to better serve the basic needs of humans.

How do you position yourselves to serve for these demands? If you ever want to participate in leading the world tomorrow, you must position yourself to attain professional skills that cultivate and nourishes science and technology today.

## 2.7  Summary

To sum it up, there are different occupations you may choose to specialise in. However, it is important to note that because of technological advancement, tremendous changes are happening in our world which will constantly affect the way we live and work. So, you will be in a good position for the changes in the future if you have a good command over technology now.

Chapter 3

# SELF-ASSESSMENT CAREER EXPLORATION

## 3.1 Introduction

This chapter includes tools that can help applicants discover the type of work activities and occupations that they would like and find exciting. It includes carrying out the following:

i. Personality test
ii. Interest test
iii. Career pathway test

For brevity, we won't cover these tests in detail here, but we will cover them extensively during the in-house training. In summary, these tests will boost your self-awareness about your personality and interests, which are key to determine the occupation you fit in.

While in Chapter 2 you were introduced to different sectors and career pathways, this chapter will help you understand what jobs you might be interested in and the ones that might suit you the most. This is important before you go on to choose university programmes, which are covered in the next chapter.

Chapter 4

# SELECTION OF COLLEGE PROGRAMME

## 4.1 Introduction

In this chapter, we describe education and training opportunities that are available in Tanzania:

   i.   Certificate programmes
   ii.  Diploma programmes
   iii. Degree programmes

There are other programmes for young people which we won't cover in this package, but we can provide them on request. These programmes are as follows:

   i.   Distance education
   ii.  Apprenticeships
   iii. Private training providers
   iv.  On-the-job training
   v.   Volunteer work

Let's begin by introducing you to different classifications of higher-education institutions in Tanzania, that you can find in different regions, before embarking on the available programmes.

## 4.2  Classification of Higher-education Institutions

Higher-education institutions in Tanzania can be classified based on their regulatory authorities. To ensure quality, higher-education institutions in Tanzania are regulated by either the National Council for Technical Education (NACTE) or Tanzania Commission for Universities (TCU).

Institutions regulated by NACTE are supposed to provide professional and technical qualifications using competence-based education at certificate, diploma and advanced diploma (equivalent to a degree) levels. On the other hand, under TCU are universities that provide qualifications at different levels, such as certificate, diploma and degree.

Different from technical institutions, academic universities around the world are mostly knowledge-based. See Table 2.4 of Chapter 2 for a brief discussion on the difference between competence and knowledge-based education.

### 4.2.1  Technical Institutions Regulated by NACTE

The NACTE report of 2020 of accredited institutions indicates that there were 582 institutions by 2020. These institutions, which are different from universities, are supposed to offer technical skills and knowledge. During the training, we will sort all the institutions according to the following:

 i. Main economic sector

 ii. Location in terms of region and district

 iii. Possible career specialisations.

The above information aims at helping Form Six leavers and equivalent applicants make informed decisions. First, it helps them understand the training institutions that are closer to their domicile; this can help them apply to the nearest institutions to save on traveling. Second, it helps them understand the probable specialisations they might consider in training institutions.

In Table 4.2, we have shown you an example of how we divide the higher-education institutions in the Dodoma region. This further shows that there are 23 higher-education institutions, most of which (almost 90%), fall under the education and health services sector. Only two are in the agriculture sector, one in ICT and one in mining, among others (see Table 4.2).

We would have done deeper analyses of higher-education institutions in every region or district in Tanzania, but for brevity, we have saved the rest for in-house training.

To facilitate your learning, we have developed an application that is accessible through our website www.tcds.or.tz. We encourage all Form Six leavers and equivalent applicants to start practising before attending our training sessions.

## 4.2.2  Universities Regulated by TCU

**TABLE 4.2:** Higher Learning Institutions in Dodoma Region

| Occupational Pathways | Colleges & University | Location |
|---|---|---|
| Agriculture | Livestock Training Agency | Mpwapwa DC |
| | Visele Live-Crop Skills Training Centre | Mpwapwa DC |
| Business Mgt & Admin. | Ngageya College of Business and Management | Dodoma MC |
| | College of Business Education | Dodoma MC |
| | Institute of Rural Development Planning | Dodoma MC |
| Gov. & Pub. Admin | Local Government Training Institute | Dodoma MC |
| Education | Mtumba Teachers' College | Dodoma MC |
| | Mpwapwa Teachers College | Mpwapwa DC |
| | Bustani Teachers College | Kondoa DC |
| | Nkuruma Mkoka Teachers College | Kongwa DC |
| | Tanzania Research and Career Development Institute | Dodoma MC |
| | St. John's University of Tanzania | Dodoma MC |
| | University of Dodoma | Dodoma MC |
| Health | City College of Health and Allied Sciences | Dodoma MC |
| | Decca College of Health and Allied Sciences | Dodoma MC |
| | Dodoma Institute of Health and Allied Sciences | Dodoma MC |
| | Int. Institute of Development and Medical Sciences | Dodoma MC |
| | Janesa Institute of Health and Allied Sciences | Dodoma MC |
| | Clinical Officers Training Centre Mvumi | Chamwino DC |
| | Mvumi Institute of Health Sciences | Chamwino DC |
| | Kondoa School of Nursing | Kondoa DC |
| ICT | Dodoma Media College | Dodoma MC |
| Mining | Polytechnic of Energy and Earth Resources Management (Madini Institute) | Dodoma MC |

Source: NACTE and Author's Analysis

In 2006, there were about 30 universities with a population of 52,831 students. By 2018, the number of universities grew to 43, with a population of more than 163,163 students (this figure comes from only 31 universities published under the universities directory on the TCU website).

Between 2013 and 2017, the number of graduates from university programmes regulated by TCU was averaged at 45,000 annually. However, this number did not include the graduates from other programmes of higher-learning institutions regulated by NACTE. The number of higher-learning institutions regulated by NACTE was about 500 in total in 2020 implies that the average number of graduates could be far beyond 45,000 if graduates from institutions regulated by NACTE are considered.

## 4.2.3 Secondary School Leavers

In 2019, the advanced secondary school graduates averaged 90,000, without taking into account the teachers' college diploma and certificate graduates, which averaged at 12,000. This implies that approximately 100,000 candidates compete for university programmes; we assume that it may have a capacity of 45,000 places for new entrants annually.

The above assumption is based on our previous calculation where we estimated that 45,000 graduates exit from the university education system annually, which may indicate that (in a steady state) the same number of vacancies will be created in the university education system.

It must be noted here that there will be fewer university vacancies compared to the candidates. Hence, there will always be advanced secondary-education leavers who will not be selected to join university programmes, even though they may have satisfied the admission criteria.

Our humble advice to A-level leavers is therefore that you must not focus with all your energy to compete for the scant university vacancies under TCU. Rather, be open-minded to other higher-learning opportunities offered by technical colleges and institutions under NACTE.

In our opinion, you might benefit more from undergoing technical training at institutions before joining university. Although this assumption holds if the technical training institutions do what they were supposed to do. The reason for this is that you will be trained on competences in technical colleges which might put you in a better position in the labour market than someone who has attained academic knowledge from universities. You can see this difference in Table 2.4 of Chapter 2.

Please note that you will not lose time in doing this; it might only make a difference of one or two years, depending on the programme you choose. However, it might be worth doing so as compared to graduating early with merely an academic degree.

## 4.3  University Programmes to Choose From

In this Section, we provided a summary of a few programmes provided by academic universities in Dodoma. For brevity reasons, we have presented only certificate courses that may be provided by these universities. We say "may be provided" because universities may stop providing some of the courses as time goes on. During the training, we aim at providing an in-depth analysis of more courses and programmes provided by all universities in different regions in Tanzania.

**TABLE 4.3:** Certificate Course Programmes at UDOM and SJUT

| Main Sector | Occupational Pathways | Course | University |
|---|---|---|---|
| Agriculture | Agriculture | Apiculture | UDOM |
| Industry | Non-manufacturing Industry | Geosciences | SJUT |
| Services | Business Mgt. and Admin. | Business Administration | SJUT |
| | Education and Training | Educational Technology | UDOM |
| | Finance | Accounting and Finance | UDOM |
| | Hospitality and Tourism | Tourism and Cultural Heritage | UDOM |
| | Human Services | Social Work and Comm. Devt. | UDOM |
| | | Medical Lab. Technology | SJUT |
| | | Science and Lab. Technology | SJUT |
| | Govt. and Public Administration | Public Administration and Mgt. | UDOM |
| | Information Technology | Information and Comm. Technology | UDOM |
| | | Journalism | UDOM |
| | | Computer Maintenance | SJUT |

Source: TCU and Author's Analysis

At the time of writing this manual, there were two main universities in Dodoma: University of Dodoma (UDOM), a public university with the capacity of more than 30,000 students, and St. John's University of Tanzania (SJUT), a private university with a capacity of 5,000–10,000 students.

Table 4.3 shows different certificate programmes that you may choose from UDOM or SJUT when you apply. This information might have changed because universities modify their offerings when it is in their best interest to do so. We have put the information below for illustration purposes only.

## 4.4 Summary

In this chapter, we have provided information about university and college programmes where we have linked them with various economic sectors. Further, we have shown what occupation and economic sectors you might end up working in if you choose a certain programme. This information is key for any youngster in deciding their future career path. In the next section, we show you how you can plan to attain your goals, which is important.

Chapter 5

# CAREER PLANNING

## 5.1 Introduction

This chapter borrows heavily from Chapter 2 of our book titled "The Future of Work in Tanzania: Preparing for the Work that Does Not Exist Yet". In the book, we talk about how planning for your career is as important as planning for any other project that requires time and money. Planning matters because it helps you achieve the following:

   i.  Using time and other resources effectively
  ii.  Focusing in the right direction
 iii.  Building a framework and measuring progress
 iv.  Assessing suitability in what you aspire to be

## 5.2 What is Career Planning

In PRINCE2, a plan is a document that describes how, when and by whom a specific target can be achieved.

These targets may include the goals you set to achieve, the time you attach to the activities to achieve these goals, the costs you set to the activities, the quality of your achievements and the benefits you derive from them.

# 5.3  Practical Steps to Plan Your Career

Planning for your career can be simplified into four steps:
    Step 1: Situational analysis
    Step 2: Set your main objective
    Step 3: Break the main objective into smaller objectives
    Step 4: Evaluate resource requirements in each stage
    Step 5: Determine the risk management strategy

## 5.3.1  Step 1: Situational Analysis

Situational analysis encompasses identifying socioeconomic problems that face society and possible occupations that can solve these problems.

For example, if malaria is one of the top-ten killer diseases in Africa, people do not necessarily need to specialise in medicine to solve the problem. Someone may be a businessman, footballer, singer or political leader and contribute to solving the same problem of malaria. Regardless of the occupation of an individual, the way they contribute to solving the problem is key. Occupation is a means to an end and not an end in itself.

Therefore, rather than asking a person what their dream is, we must ask what problem they are passionate about solving. This will lead youngsters to correctly determine the occupations which they can specialise in, in order to solve socio-economic problems. Alternatively, we may ask "what problem would you like to solve" instead of what they want to be when they grow up.

Young people should therefore not be driven by what the occupation pays but rather the extent of sustainability of such an occupation in addressing current and future problems that impact the society. They shouldn't spend a lot of time thinking about money; rather, they ought to think about problems and their solutions in an innovative way.

## 5.3.2  Step 2: Set Big and Specific Objectives

The second step in planning is to determine what you want to achieve in the longer term based on the results from the situational analysis. For example, if you are passionate about reducing malaria morbidity and mortality in your country, your big goal might be "A country free from malaria morbidity and mortality". Since you cannot achieve the big goal on your own, you will need to mobilise other stakeholders to join you in addressing it.

After developing a big objective, you will need to break it down into specific objectives, which will further contribute in achieving a big goal. These objectives need to be specific, measurable, realistic, attainable and time-bound.

Further, if you already have a career plan, you will have to review specific objectives. But, if you have never done this before, now is the time to develop a plan and the specific objects as well.

One thing to remember is when developing specific objectives, you need to select the occupation(s) that will increase the likelihood of addressing a problem based on the current and future realities. It's good to understand that you may have more than one occupation. For example, if your big goal is "A country free of malaria morbidity and mortality", your specific objectives might be as follows:

   i.   To graduate with an economics degree from Harvard University by 2023; or

  ii.   To graduate in medicine from Muhimbili University by 2025.

Specific objectives need to be holistic, focusing on all key skills required to perform work.

## 5.3.3  Step 3: Break the Specific Objectives into Activities

After developing your specific objectives, it is time to translate those into implementable activities. These activities will depend on the time frame of when the objective is expected to be achieved.

Our organisation encourages caregivers to educate their children on career planning as early as possible. This builds a strong foundation for children as they can then update their plans to suit the need of the time.

For example, if you chose to graduate at 21 years (your specific objective), you may divide these years into 5 + 7 + 6 + 3, where the first 5 years are for pre-primary, 7 years for primary school, 6 years for secondary school and 3 years for university. Assuming you have already passed 6 years of secondary school, your planning will focus on the 3 years of university onwards, as shown in Figure 5.3.

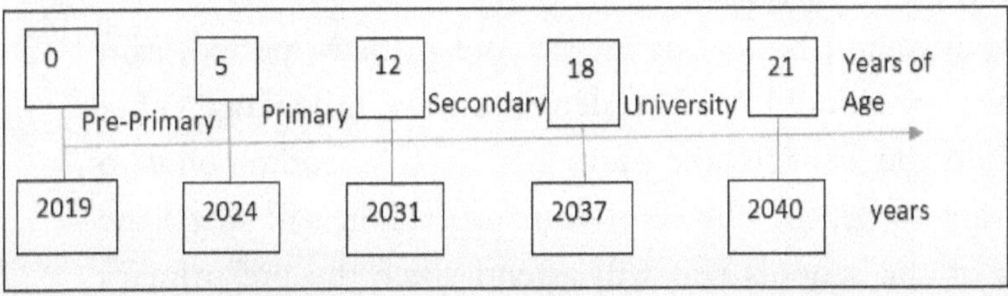


**FIGURE 5.3** Career Planning for 0-21 Years

From the above specific objective, the following activities can be done while planning for the university stage:

    i. Apply for admission and degree course programme registration;

    ii. Apply for financial assistance (loan from HESLB);

    iii. Learn university study skills such as metacognition;

    iv. Take core and optional courses as per the curriculum;

    v. Take tests and exams as per the almanac.

## 5.3.4 Step 4: Evaluate Resource Requirements in Each Stage.

Following the breaking down of the big objective into smaller targets, you will need to determine the activities to undertake in each stage and the number of resources needed for that purpose.

This step is different than the first and second stages in various ways. It is formed at the end of each stage before the next stage begins. Unlike the first and second steps, this step is more detailed because it is closer to the period where activities take place.

At this point, the planner has more information on what needs to be done than the first two steps. It should be noted that the caregiver is a custodian to facilitate career planning during the early years. So, caregivers need to play a key role in facilitating this process.

For instance, budgeting in the pre-primary period, as a caregiver, you would need to decide on the following: What school do you want to take your child to? (Depending on who they want to be, the choice of your profession will shape the choice of the schools you will attend since the pre-primary stage); How far is the school from your house? (If the school is not in your proximity, you might consider relocating or arrange for private transport. If you cannot be able to take your children to school, you will need to arrange someone to do it for you).

Other aspects of planning in each stage will be elaborated during the training. For example, we will explain what sort of competences you will plan to attain. You may also consult the Tanzanite Career Development Services (TCDS; www.tcds.or.tz) for coaching on career planning and to familiarise yourself with other career services.

## 5.3.5 Step 5: Determine the Risk Management Strategy.

To be successful in your career, you will need to identify, assess and control the risks which may hamper your success. A risk is defined (in PRINCE2) as an uncertain event or a set of events that, should they happen, will affect the achievement of the objectives.

One of the major risks in career planning may be the lack of financial resources: i.e. the loss of a sponsor's source of income due to redundancy, retirement, illness, total incapacitation, accidents and other reasons. Other risks include the death of a parent who was the main breadwinner of the family.

These and other such events, if not managed well, might hamper the achievement of your career goals. It is naive to plan your career with the assumption that everything will run smoothly.

If you wish for your career to run smoothly, you might end up disappointed. The world changes very fast and moves in indeterministic ways, and these changes come with risks. It's better to be informed and prepare for them. Those who are able to match their speed to the pace of the changing world prosper.

# 5.4  How to Execute Your Plan?

## 5.4.1  Implement by Stages

Implementation by stages enables you to monitor and evaluate your progress easily. I once read a story online about climbers of Mt. Kilimanjaro, the tallest mountain in Africa. In this testimony, the climber had to take 128,263 steps to reach the highest point. He made it to the top "one step at a time". There would be no other way for him to make it to the top but by taking one step at a time! This is the crux of venturing into any new challenge: one step at a time.

You might have also heard of the ancient expression "Rome was not built in a day", which simply means that it takes time to create things of great value. This is a natural law for those who aim high for their future. So, to implement your career plans, you need to break it into small stages which you can master one after the other.

# 5.5  Summary

As we conclude this section, an exercise is given to help you practice planning for your three years of undergraduate studies. Start by studying the figure below that shows a long-term plan for someone born in 2019 to become a macro-economist by the age of 21. Extend it to cover postgraduate study up to the master's level.

| A DRAFT PLAN FOR A CHILD BORN IN 2019 BECOME A PROMINENT MACROECONOMIST IN 2040 (AT THE AGE OF 21). | | | | | | | | |
| --- | --- | --- | --- | --- | --- | --- | --- | --- |
| no | Objective | Target | Activity Description | Inputs | Estimated Cost (TSh.) | Responsible Persons (Responsibilities) | | |
| | | | | | | Parents | Teachers | Mentor/Advisor |
| 1 | To become a Professional Macro-economist when I turn 21 in 2040. | To Earn First degree Certificate in (Economics) by the age of 21 in 2040. | Enroll Into Pre-Primary School between (Age 1-5) | 1. Pre-schoool | | | | |
| | | | | 2. School Bus | | | | |
| | | | | 3. Learning Materials | | | | |
| | | | Enroll Into Primary School Between (Age 6-12) | 1. Primary schoool | | | | |
| | | | | 2. School Bus | | | | |
| | | | | 3. Learning Materials | | | | |
| | | | To Complete Secondary School Between (Age 13-18) | 1. Secondary schoool | | | | |
| | | | | 2. School Bus | | | | |
| | | | | 3. Learning Materials | | | | |
| | | | University (Age 19-21) | 1. University | | | | |
| | | | | 2. School Bus | | | | |
| | | | | 3. Learning Materials | | | | |

**FIGURE 5.5** Planning Exercise

The activities in the draft plan have been set in 5-year periods for pre-primary, 7 years for primary school, 6 years for secondary school and 3 years for university.

As part of this exercise, you must do the following:

1. Fill in the estimated cost for each of the activities;

2. Develop a short-term plan for each year of the named activities. (for example, the "Age 1–5 Plan" is a general one because it covers almost 5 years. Your role is to break it down in a detailed annual plan.

3. Extend it (add another target) to incorporate a plan for your master's degree.

Chapter 6

# ADMISSION INFORMATION

## 6.1  Introduction

I f you have mastered Chapter 5, this chapter will be a revision of the same. We will introduce you to undergraduate admission criteria and the application timelines as well as where, how and when to apply.

## 6.2  Meeting Admission Criteria

Entry requirements differ depending on your background. Form Six leavers are evaluated differently from ordinary diploma holders. TCU prepares the Undergraduate Admission Guide wherein all undergraduate programmes offered by all higher-learning institutions regulated by TCU are listed in one place along with the criteria.

### 6.2.1  Criteria for Form Six Applicants

We advise you to visit the TCU website and download the "Admission Guidebook for Form Six Applicants".

TCU stipulates that no Form Six applicant should be admitted to any undergraduate programme unless they have at least 4.0 points in at least two subjects (where A = 5, B = 4, C = 3, D = 2, E = 1).

So, if your points are below 4.0, you do not satisfy the minimum requirement. In that case, you must decide to apply to do certificate or diploma courses before you re-apply to the undergraduate programme (see Chapter 4). However, each specific programme has additional requirements, which may be higher than 4.0 points. Read the guidebook for more details. Notably, most degree programmes in medical health require at least 6 to 8 points. The Doctor of Medicine (MD) requires a minimum of 8 entry points in Physics, Chemistry and Biology, whereas, the Bachelor of Science in Nursing (BScN) requires a minimum of 6 entry points with three principal passes in Physics, Chemistry and Biology.

## 6.2.2 Criteria for Certificates and Ordinary Diploma Holders

We urge you to visit the TCU website and download the "Admission Guide Book for Ordinary Diploma/Equivalent Applicants" for reference with this section.

The minimum requirements are a Full Technician Certificate (FTC) with an average of C, (where A = 5, B = 4, C = 3, D = 2 points) or at least a GPA of 3.0 ordinary diploma (NTA Level 6).

# 6.3 Your Application Package

Your application package will require some of your basic documents in soft copy. Hence, prepare these important documents, certify them from any Notary Public or Commissioner of Oaths and have them scanned (in colour) and store them as soft copies. You will need to store them online so that you can access them at any time.

These documents include the following:

    i.  Birth certificates

    ii.  National Identification Card (NIDA)

    iii.  All certificates and transcripts of your background studies

    iv.  Death certificates (if applicable), and

    v.  Register your personal email account

Note: This list is not exhaustive.

## 6.4 Application Procedures

Application procedures start with the following:

1. Deciding what you would like to be (as discussed in Chapter 4; please read it thoroughly before proceeding).
2. Searching for suitable programmes based on your academic background and your ambition.
3. Finding out about undergraduate admission requirements.
4. Knowing when, where and how to apply.

### 6.4.1 When to Apply

Normally, the TCU and the universities will announce the offerings for the courses any time they wish to. We thus advise you to refer to "Table 3: Calendar for 2019/2020 Admission Cycle" available online at www.tcu.go.tz under undergraduate Admission Guidebooks. You may wish to download the pdf file named "Revised 2019/20 Undergraduate Admission Guide Book for Form Six or Equivalent Applicants" for more information on the admission dates.

**TABLE 6.4:** Probable Undergraduate Admission Timetable for 2020

| S.N. | Date | Activity |
|---|---|---|
|  | **1ˢᵗ May–30ᵗʰ August 2020** | **TCDS IN-HOUSE TRAININGS** |
| 1. | 24ᵗʰ June | Mini-application window opens for applicants from previous years. |
| 2. | 15ᵗʰ July | The major application and Admission window opens for all. |
| 3. | 10ᵗʰ August | Deadline for first round of applications. |
| 4. | 11ᵗʰ–15ᵗʰ August | Submission of students admitted in the first round to TCU |
| 5. | 20ᵗʰ August | Announcement of students admitted in the first round of applications. |

Source: TCU and Author's Analysis

From the 2019/20 admission timetable, we think that applications for undergraduate admission will be open in late June 2020. For that reason, we have scheduled our in-house training starting from 1st May to August 2020. You are therefore advised to visit our website at TCDS to know the nearby city where the training will take place.

The dates and months in Table 6.4 are for illustration purposes as they were taken from the year 2019/20. However, this may change in the future. For instance, due to the Coronavirus (COVID-19) outbreak in March 2020, many learning institutions were ordered to stop classes. The closure will probably affect the normal graduation and admission circles as well.

All else being constant, the application period for admission to most higher-learning institutions normally spans from May to September annually. So, you must be on the lookout and regularly visit the websites of the universities of your preference for updates on calls for applications.

## 6.4.2 Where to Apply

Submit your application directly to the university of your preference.

## 6.4.3 How to Apply

There are three ways to submit your application:

Physical submission of hard copies of the forms to the university admission office or sending your application kit through the post office or through "Online Application and Admission System".

The first two above-mentioned ways are becoming less popular nowadays due to the advancement in communication technology and the use of the internet. Instead, the online application system is dominating in university applications and admissions systems. In the future, every application for admission will likely be done online. This calls for you to learn how to use the internet.

## 6.4.4 Re-application & Appeal or Transfer

Sometimes you might want to change your programme/ course or even university. This is still possible. There are various reasons which may justify you to do so, such as health, environment, cost or change of future career plans. Do not get stuck to the programme you are not happy with or you do not see a future in.

In case you are enrolled in one university and you reach the decision to change a programme and university, you will be required to fill the (Re-application Form) which can be downloaded from the TCU website before you apply for a new programme at another university of your choice.

It is important that you satisfy the minimum requirements for the course you would like to transfer or reapply to before you cancel your current course programme. This is because re-admission in any programme is subject to the same admission criteria.

## 6.5 Summary

In this chapter, we showed that university application for admission may be a very simple and easy exercise if youngsters are trained in determining what they would like to pursue. It can shape your choice of a university programme and make close monitoring of where, when and how to apply possible. However, after you are admitted to any undergraduate programme, there will be another challenge to encounter: financial costs. For this purpose, we introduce you to Financial Assistance Information in the next chapter.

Chapter 7

# FINANCIAL ASSISTANCE INFORMATION

## 7.1 Introduction

Unfortunately, university education is not free. You will have to incur a substantial amount of money throughout your training. There are three main ways to finance your studies:

i. Pay from your own or your parents' pocket.

ii. Take a loan from the Tanzania High Education Students' Loan Board (HESLB) or commercial banks.

iii. Scholarships

It is advisable to pay for the studies from your pocket if you are able to as taking a loan from commercial banks or HESLB will have long-term financial liabilities.

We have explained each of these different modes of financing below.

# 7.2 Student Loan Programmes

Compared to commercial banks, the HESLB is a reliable government body to offer financial assistance to youngsters who cannot finance their studies from their own pockets.

The main challenge is that the number of applicants is increasing to the extent that the HESLB may be overpowered soon. When that time comes, other financial institutions such as commercial banks will chip in to bridge that gap.

While the government has to educate their youngsters, the commercial banks have an additional motive for profit-making. Hence you would expect the cost of repaying the loan is higher in commercial banks than in HESLB. In case you would like to apply for HESLB, this information may be of good assistance.

## 7.2.1 Applying for Loan from HESLB

Application for a student loan from HESLB is done at the institution itself. Other information regarding HESLB can be found from the universities when you apply for admission. We advise you to visit their website www.heslb.go.tz to learn about the following:

i. **The application requirements:** Refer to the guidelines published the HESLB website www.olas.heslb.go.tz/glines for more information on:

ii. **When to apply:** For 2019/20, the loan application window was opened on June 15th, 2019 through August 15th, 2019. A list of successful loan applicants with their corresponding allocations was published on the website around 25th October 2019.

iii. **Where to apply:** You can apply directly on the HESLB website. Read the guidelines for more info at www.olas.heslb.go.tz/glines

iv. **How to apply:** All loan applications are done through the Online Loan Application and Management System (OLAMS).

Please note that these procedures are similar to those discussed in Chapter 6, Section 6.4.

One point to remember is that you will have to repay this loan later after you graduate and start working. The challenge for the government is when a big number of youngsters go jobless after graduation. This is the time when the programme can become unsustainable.

So, to make the HESLB, sustainable graduates must get employment after graduation or can employ themselves. This is why we are trying to advocate for a change in the education system so that graduates are equipped with the skills to be able to employ themselves right after graduation.

## 7.3 Scholarships

In case you cannot secure a loan from commercial banks or HESLB, you can still finance your studies through scholarships. These are financial assistance provided by different organisations in the country or even from another one. For them, their financial assistance is free: you will not be required to repay it. However, you do have to show them that you are worthy of being awarded a scholarship.

We have dedicated a whole chapter to teach you skills on how you can apply and win a scholarship in our book called "The Future of Work: Preparing for the Work that Does Not Exist Yet". You may visit our website at www.tcds.or.tz to get more information. Additionally, we also do in-house training on scholarship applications at various locations, which will be published on our website.

Just to give you a taste of our book, in Chapter 3, dedicated to "How to Apply For and Win a Scholarship", we talk about the following:

1. Your Response to Key Questions:
   a. What do you want to do?
   b. Why did you choose this university?
   c. Why do you want to do this research?
2. How to write a winning Research Proposal?
3. How to review the Literature, and
4. The importance of Referees.

Acquiring the skills for applying and receiving a scholarship when you are still young is very crucial. It might serve you to win competitive scholarships worldwide and help you achieve your goals, which you might not be able to do without a scholarship.

## 7.4  Financial Planning and Debt Management

Unless you get a scholarship, all other financial assistances have a lifelong financial obligation to repay. Since you will be liable to pay, you must plan on how you will do this.

For example, the HESLB guideline requires that repayment should be upon completion or termination from higher-education studies, where a beneficiary shall be required to repay their loan through monthly deductions of not less than 15% of their salary. Whereas, the amount payable by a self-employed beneficiary shall not be less than 100,000 per month.

In case of failing to repay in time, there are penalties: a beneficiary who fails to repay after the expiration of grace period of 24 months after graduation shall be charged a 10% one-time penalty.

Therefore, this calls for you to have a financial plan for debt management. In Chapter 4 of this manual, we talked about how you can make a plan. You may employ the same skills to plan how you will manage to repay the loan.

Alternatively, you may look for a mentor or a coach to assist you to come through with this. If you still struggle, you may consult TCDS for further assistance on this issue.

## 7.5 Summary

In this chapter, we introduced you to different sources of financial assistance to help you undertake your undergraduate studies. These sources include your parents' money, government student loans, commercial bank loans and scholarships. Among all these sources, only scholarships do not have a lifelong liability. Hence, we advise our youngsters to do develop skills in how to apply for and receive scholarships to increase their chances to fund their studies and future career.

# ANNEX: EXERCISES

On the last day of our in-house training, we will spend time practising career planning and filling up college applications. Our exercises will aim at building competencies in planning for your careers and seeing whether you can apply for college admission without any assistance.

We will ask you the questions on:

i. **Developing or Reviewing Career Planning**
We will ask candidates to practice career planning. They will have to present their plans in a plenary.

ii. **Filling up College Application**
We will ask candidates to practice filling up applications for college admission and present their work in a plenary.

# BIBLIOGRAPHY

Borgonovo, Alfred, Brian Friedrich, and Michael Wells (2019). *Competency-Based Accounting Education, Training, and Certification: An Implementation Guide*. The World Bank.

United Nations Statistical Division et al. (2008). *International Standard Industrial Classification of All Economic Activities (ISIC)*. 4. United Nations Publications.

International Labour Office (2012). *International Standard Classification of Occupations 2008 (ISCO-08): Structure, group definitions and correspondence tables*. International Labour Office

# ABOUT THE AUTHOR

Dr Pancras K. Mayengo (Ph.D.) is a certified PRINCE2 practitioner in Project Management. He holds BSc, MA, MSc and a Ph.D. in Economics from the University of Essex, UK. He has won five Ph.D. scholarships from various esteemed universities around the world.

He previously worked in academia as an Assistant Lecturer before joining the government mainstream workforce as an Economist. He also worked with the World Bank's Macroeconomics, Trade and Investment (MTI) Global Practice in Tanzania.

www.ingramcontent.com/pod-product-compliance
Lightning Source LLC
Chambersburg PA
CBHW021347060726
47591CB00006B/2204